The Dragon Egg Quest

Written by Shareen Wilkinson
and Marcus Wilkinson

Illustrated by Michael Emmerson

Collins

Elbron was in the garden when he spotted the dragon egg.

It was spinning down the hill into town.

3

Elbron gulped. The egg belonged to a big red dragon.

If the dragon went into town to look for it, she might demolish the town with a flick of her tail!

Elbron's sister Andra spotted the egg too.

"We must return it to the dragon, to stop her getting near town!" Andra yelled.

Elbron and Andra sprinted down the road,
but the egg had vanished.

"Now what?" panted Andra.

"Look!" grinned Elbron, spotting a track in the dust. "The egg went down here!"

The children sped off. The egg track led to a pit full of mud.

In the midst of the mud was an abandoned griffin's nest.

The dragon's egg slid down into the nest.
Andra slid across the mud to get it.

Andra handed the egg to Elbron. The shell was cracking!

"Quick!" yelped Elbron. "We must get it back to its nest!"

The children sprinted to the hilltop, and left the egg by the dragon's nest. The dragon peeked out.

At that second, the eggshell split! The little dragon was born.

In a dragon nest

eggs

flints

twigs

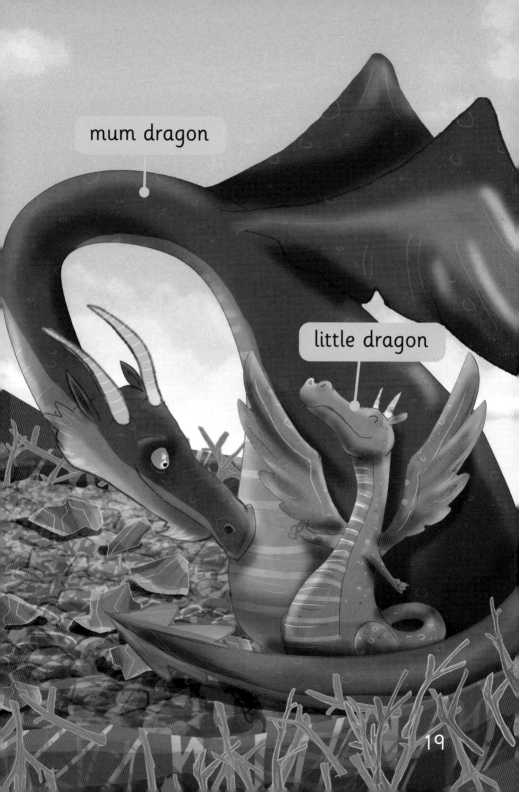

To Andra and
Elbron
with thanks

Map

Review: After reading

Use your assessment from hearing the children read to choose any GPCs, words or tricky words that need additional practice.

Read 1: Decoding
- Focus on longer words with adjacent consonants. Ask the children to read the following aloud using the chunking method.
  spinn/ing dem/ol/ish El/bron And/ra a/band/oned sprint/ed
- Model reading page 2 fluently. Challenge the children to read page 3 fluently. Say: Can you blend in your head when you read these words?
- Bonus content: Ask the children to read the labels on pages 18 and 19. Say: Can you describe the scene using these words and other words you have read in the book? (e.g. *flick, tail, spotted, midst, slid, pit, cracking*)

Read 2: Prosody
- Ask the children to work in pairs to practise reading pages 14 and 15, using a storyteller voice to create suspense and excitement.
- Remind them to think about tone, pace and which words to emphasise. Ask: What sort of voice will you choose for Elbron?
- Let children take turns to read a page aloud, and discuss their decisions and the effects.

Read 3: Comprehension
- Encourage the children to compare the story with other dragon stories, or stories about eggs, they have read or heard. Ask: Which did you prefer and why?
- Point to **Quest** in the title. Ask: What is a quest? (e.g. *a hunt or a journey in search for something*) Ask: In what way was the story a quest? (e.g. *the children searched for the egg*)
- Point to the word **spotted** on page 2. Say: This word can mean different things. What does it mean here? (*noticed/saw*) How do you know? (e.g. *because it isn't describing something, so can't be spotted – as in patterned with dots*)
- Turn to pages 22 and 23. Ask the children to retell the story of their search for the egg, using the map. Prompt with questions. Ask:
  - o Where did the story start? (*by the house on the hill*) What was the egg doing? (*spinning down the hill*)
  - o What clue did the children find that showed where the egg went? (*a track*)
  - o Where did the egg roll next? (*into a griffin's nest*)
- Bonus content: Use pages 20 and 21 to prompt children to think of another story about the children and the dragon. Ask: What happened next? Were the wings magical?